PORTRAIT

OF LATIN AMERICA

A collection of photographs to
celebrate ten years of working and
travelling in Latin America

Mo Fini

TUMI

First published by Tumi (publications) 1990
Distributed by Tumi Latin American Craft Centres
8/9 New Bond Street Place, Bath, Avon BA1 1BH, England
Tel (0225) 462367/480470 Fax (0225) 444870 Telex 449212 Lantel G

Text and photography © M. S. Fini 1990
© Photographs: page 9 J. Fini; pages 11, 12 L. Davies; backcover J. Etchart
Text and photographs compiled by L. Davies
Layout by J. Andrews at A.D.S. Ltd, Bristol, England
Printed by Butler & Tanner Ltd, Frome, England.

ISBN 0-9511055-1-5

Caption overleaf:
Fiesta de la Cruz, Huancané, Peru.

This book is dedicated to all the families and individuals all over Latin America who, during a decade of travelling, have given me their assistance, their love and their generous hospitality. Among the many thousands of people who have inspired my admiration over the years, there are a few who deserve special thanks, not least those friends who have become the subjects, sometimes unwittingly, of my photographs. I have collected together these images as a way of expressing my gratitude to all of Latin America, from the children who have offered their smiles, to the elderly who have offered their wisdom.

Ecuador:
Antonio, Segundo, Rafael and Alberto Morales and their respective families (Agato Community near Otavalo); Rafael Chiza (Otavalo); Pablo Vera (Cuenca); Samuel Quinatua (Puyo).

Peru:
The García family, Señor and Señora Baldeón, the people of Kamaq Maki cooperative (Huancayo); the weavers of Santa Ana, Señora Seville (Ayacucho); Señor and Señora Palomino (San Pedro de Cajas); Artesanía Shipibo (Pucalpa); our godson Carlos Llamoca and his family (Cuzco); Sebastián Quinto, Florentino Quispe, Placido and Ruth Quillo (Pisac); Joaquim Quispe and his family (Juliaca); all the people of Taquile Island especially our two godchildren, Alejandro Flores Huatta and his family, Señor Yucra, Gerardo Huatta and his family.

Chile:
Eduardo and his family (Santiago); Roberto Monsalve (Villarica).

Bolivia:
Feli and her children and the many musicians I know in La Paz.

Mexico:
María and José Padilla, Estéban de la O Ibarra, Landores family, Fortunado Jimón and his family, the glass blowers of Vidrio Típico Tonalá, Felipe Días, Miguel Alvarez, Alejandra Jimón, Andres Lucano, Clemente Luna (Guadalajara); the Padilla family, Andres Galindo and his family, El Arte Maya, Juventino Lopez, Mario Cortés, Cresenciano Candía, Luis Gutiérrez, José Luis de la Rosa (Mexico City); Guadalupe León García (Oaxaca); Victor and Gabriel Rodríguez Pereyra, Fidel Gutiérrez and especially Señor Jorge Castañeda and his family (Taxco).

Guatemala:
Juan Ventura Tol and his family, Señora Tol Ren (Chichicastenango); the people of Santiago and San Pedro (Atitlán).

Special thanks to the spirits of Papa and Mama Quinto.

MEXICO

BELIZE

GUATE
MALA HONDURAS

EL
SALVADOR NICARAGUA

COSTA RICA PANAMA

ATLANTIC

OCEAN

Caracas

VENEZUELA

Georgetown
Paramaribo
GUYANA Cayenne
Bogota SURINAM
FRENCH
COLOMBIA GUYANA

ECUADOR Quito
Guayaquil
Iquitos

PERU

Cajamarca

Huanuco

BRAZIL

Lima

Machu Picchu
Cuzco BOLIVIA
Lake Titicaca
La Paz Brasilia
Cochabamba

Sucre

PACIFIC

PARAGUAY

OCEAN

Asuncion

Santiago
URUGUAY
Buenos Aires
CHILE Montevideo

ARGENTINA

PREFACE

These photographs are a way of introducing the extraordinary communities and individuals I have come to know, love and work with during a decade of travelling in Latin America – and the book is designed to give the full story behind Tumi without saying it all in words.

Since Tumi started in 1978 with a sackful of Peruvian sweaters and a market stall in London's Camden Town, it has grown to become a successful retail enterprise specialising in traditional Latin American crafts; ranging from hand-woven textiles and decorative pottery to Mexican silver and alpaca woollens. Tumi encompasses everything that the Latin American artisan has to offer, from Andean music to Ayacucho rugs, and to me it is a celebration of their rich cultural heritage.

Today Tumi trades with nine countries and relies on the skilled craftsmanship of hundreds of families. People who, in turn, have come to depend on Tumi and the demand in the West for their unique artefacts, for their financial independence and self-respect.

I have developed a close working relationship with many of these communities and I visit them at least once a year. We sleep on the same floor and together we thank Mother Earth before we share the same simple meal.

Our relationship is based on a harmonious socio-economic phenomenon which is built on love, faith and understanding of one another. Not only do I find myself at the head of a company, but also at the head of what I regard as a large family. While encouraging them to rediscover and maintain the roots of their traditional craftsmanship, I participate in their happiness, their marriages, festivals, births and baptisms. I know all their problems and suffer with them, often adding my own to theirs.

I am often asked how I cope with living half my life in Latin America and the other half in the UK. My answer to this is very simple: 'The West drives me mad and discharges me and the people of Latin America revitalise me. That is the secret of how I survive.'

Since my first journey to Latin America in 1978, I have travelled extensively through Central and Southern American countries – my mode of transport has varied from foot and donkey to truck, bus and plane. In this vast sub-continent of contrasting landscapes, I have found hunger, despair and conflict; I have discovered too, among deserts, forests, magnificent mountains and ancient ruins, the warmth, resilience and great hope of the Latin American people.

This collection of images sets out to show some of the faces and landscapes which have made the greatest impact on my life. Notwithstanding the title, it by no means covers the whole of Latin America; the book merely concentrates on those countries in which I have worked the longest and with which I have the strongest links.

Mo Fini, June 1990

INTRODUCTION

In June 1978, after finishing a degree in Business and Industrial Relations, I sold my old BSA motorbike for a few hundred pounds and set off with my wife, Jane, for Bogotá in Colombia.

I decided that my Nikomat camera, which my brother had sent me from Japan to replace an old Zenith E which had been stolen in Yugoslavia in 1973, was far too heavy and bulky for the journey. So I spent some of the travelling funds on an Olympus compact camera which slid easily into the side of my rucksack.

Bogotá was a much more dangerous place than I had imagined. By the time we had booked into a two-dollar room in the poor area of the city, I had already had my jeans stolen from my rucksack. Our aim was to travel for as long as possible with the $1,000 (US) that we jointly owned, so our budget was very tight. The third night of our trip, however, ended up being cheaper than we'd bargained for: we spent the night in a police cell.

Neither of us spoke a word of Spanish. I knew from a Bob Dylan song that *Señor* meant Mr and, from the old John Wayne films, that *hombre* meant man. Hence, to this day, I am still not sure for what offence we were being held. I do remember that, after a lot of hassles, they forced me up against the wall, pressed a sub-machine gun hard into my stomach and pulled the trigger. I felt the holes in my stomach and was about to fall to the ground when I realised that the gun had been empty.

I heard a word like 'cocaine', from a long sentence in Spanish. And hours later I heard that, as the first accusation didn't stick, I was now charged with being a member of the guerilla force M19....

When eventually they let us go, we took the next bus south and spent several days in San Agustín, a beautiful village, and then hurried on towards Ecuador. It was a great relief to leave Colombia, and travelling in Ecuador seemed comparatively easy until we got stuck in the

After fixing our rucksacks to the donkey, using my long scarf, we set off on a long journey along the Huascarán path. Lake Llanganuco near Huaráz, Peru, December 1978.

middle of the *Amazonas*. For several weeks we were abandoned (three of us this time) in the jungle. We had originally gone for the day, but after an offer of hospitality from a *mestizo* we decided to stay longer. The following day he left for a day-trip in his canoe – and never returned.

We exchanged almost all our possessions for food from a nearby tribe. Tired of eating green bananas, crocodile meat, large wood beetle and dry monkey meat, we decided to take a big risk – we set off following a narrow jungle path, just hoping for the best. If you dislike snakes as much as I do then the Amazon is not the place to be. And my attempt to catch a fish in the shallow river brought a snake to the end of my hook....

Several months later, we were trying to hitch a ride to Peru. In Ecuador it was easy, but to Peruvians, a thumb in the air was more of a rude gesture than anything else and when they did stop they tried to charge us before they even asked where we wanted to go.

After weeks of camping by a beach near Zorritos in northern Peru, we got lucky and hitched a ride to Trujillo on the back of a large Volvo truck which was returning empty from Ecuador. We had to sit on a wide platform and hold on tight to our things so they couldn't fall over the side.

Days later we got another lift to Chimbote, heading for Huaráz in the mountains. This time the driver kindly let us ride in the cabin while our rucksacks were left on the back of the truck. On the way, we stopped and gave a lift to a local man who got off somewhere before us. When our driver pulled away, I felt the side-pocket of my rucksack to find that all the films I had taken had been stolen. I remembered the face of the man who was sitting on the back. He suddenly looked so horrible in my thoughts that I think I could have killed him. All the pictures of Colombia and the *Amazonas*, they were gone.

From Chimbote we travelled east to the mountain of Huaráz. From there we climbed to Huazcarán, an elegant peak which, at 6,768 metres, is the third highest mountain in South America. The first night we camped at the side of Lake Llanganuco, just below the peaks. Our Peruvian companion, Carlos, tried hard to understand the few words of Spanish we had picked up. As I made special efforts to learn the language as fast as I could, I began to feel more at home here than I had ever felt in all my 15 years in Britain.

I had never really come to terms with the British reserve. Here in South America, things were different – people would joke and laugh, they would embrace you and, if they were as nice as our friend Carlos, they would share with you the few small trout they had caught from the lake. And the hot, dry landscapes we had seen reminded me of my childhood and the desert of Kashan in Central Persia.

We stayed at Lake Llanganuco long enough to adapt to the altitude and then one night, while sitting around our camp fire, I asked Carlos: What goes on beyond the mountains? He told us that several communities lived on the other side. If we had a mule, he said, we could get there in three days. But we had no mule. You could buy a donkey, he said. But where from?

Leaving Lima for Santiago in the back of a truck carrying lead balls. January 1979.

Early the next morning, he brought us a donkey which, judging by the state of its hooves, had not been used for some time. We paid $5.00 (US) for the animal and set off on a remarkable journey – a journey which was to become one of the landmarks of all my years of travelling.

In November 1978, we reached Lima. Our movements were restricted by limited funds; after we parted with the donkey, we travelled on foot or, if lucky, on the back of a truck.

The long desert route from Lima to Chile proved a difficult and uncomfortable journey. We got a lift in a slow truck carrying large lead balls. Its top speed was 20 miles per hour. The Atacama desert temperature reached 40°C. We had no water and the cabin separated us from the driver, making communication difficult. It took us 12 days to reach Santiago in Chile.

It was another six months before we approached Peru again – this time from the Bolivian side. In the meantime, we had travelled to southern Chile and got stuck in the no-man's-land between Argentina and Chile. The two countries were at war with each other and we found our-

9

selves right in the middle of it all. After continuing on to Argentina, it took us some time to reach Bolivia, mostly travelling on meat trucks.

The Peruvian Andes were not as hostile as the desert. The snow-covered mountain peaks gave way to deep valleys inhabitated largely by Aymara and Quechua Indians. My origins are among textile people, and it became my strength to find here, in Cuzco and the surrounding valleys, the intricate hand-woven textiles of these ancient and simple people. I would stare for hours at their exquisite work. Our long stay in the Andes left me with a strong and lasting impression of life.

Around this time, we made several trekking explorations – including a walk from Cuzco to the lost city of the Incas that must have taken us over two weeks, during which we refuelled only once with supplies.

This journey took us from Cuzco along the Inca route to Chinchero village, where we camped facing the peaks of Maras under a full moon. At this height the temperature fell below freezing, but our fire kept us warm. From out here we descended to Calca and, several days later, we followed the Inca route through the Sacred Valley of the Incas to our final destination, Machupicchu (page 30).

With great regret we left Peru and returned to the United Kingdom. Jane embarked on a post-graduate course, but I found myself totally unable to adjust to the English way of life. Suddenly everything seemed so complicated. While we were travelling life had perhaps been far too simple. We had existed – at subsistence level – for a year on as little as £800, but now we were home and had plenty of food, I found to my surprise that living in a 'civilised' country did not make me happy.

I was unable to contemplate joining a factory, an office or even wearing a suit and tie. It was all too formal for me. I could not escape my thoughts of South America, or the pain of leaving it behind. Our return seemed too much for me to handle. I had left a land and a people that I loved. And, on the streets of London, I felt lost.

As we walked around Lake Titicaca we searched for knitters who would sit by the lake herding their llamas, always carrying a drop spindle to spin wool as they were walking and a pair of push bike spokes to knit with when they were sitting down.

I don't remember exactly how, but I managed to raise some money for a return ticket. With a few hundred pounds, my old portable camera and my rucksack, I went back to Peru. This time alone.

In Juliaca, a town close to Lake Titicaca on the Peruvian border, I didn't feel inclined to hang around. Rising from the *altiplano*, the city is filthy and dusty. Apparently, they forgot to put in any sewers before they built the houses. It is like one enormous public lavatory and, when it rains, the city literally joins Lake Titicaca, about ten kilometres away. Juliaca was a small village until the 1960s when a population explosion swelled its size; and its position close to the *altiplano* breeding areas of the llama and alpaca contributed to its development as a commercial centre for wool and skin products.

When I arrived there in the late 1970s, there were large warehouses belonging to big companies. They bought the wool from the peasants and transported it to Arequipa where it was spun ready for export to America, Europe or Japan. It seemed ludicrous to me that a town in which one out of every two people was unemployed, sold its raw material (which could alleviate much of its own misery and create jobs for many of its own people) to the industrial world. In exchange, man-made fibres and analine dyes were sold back to them at twice the price.

I met a man there by the name of Señor Quispe who took me round and showed me the town. One Monday morning I went with him to the weekly market. It was 4.00 am, and the idea was to buy parts of knitted sweaters from both Quechua and Aymara settlers of the *altiplano* so that my friend's wife could sew them together and sell them in Puno market to tourists.

I asked Señor Quispe to buy enough to make a number of sweaters for me. He was astonished by this idea, but I assured him that I was serious and a quick calculation convinced me that I could afford to buy between 50 and 60 sweaters, leaving me with enough money to get back to Lima. We both returned, happier, with two saddle bags loaded with sweaters.

Two weeks later I was sleeping on top of my sweaters on the docks at Callao port waiting for the Pacific Steam Navigation Company who were sailing with my goods. I carried the sacks on my shoulder and, leaving them just above the main decks, I flew back to Britain. And it was here, with these modest imports, that the story of Tumi began.

Two years after the birth of Tumi, we had made considerable commercial losses. My debt to the bank was increasing even though I was

It is customary after a ceremony, for the godfather to divide roasted guinea pig among the relatives.

After the baptism of my 10th godchild. Left to right: grandfather and grandmother; Rosemaria (mother); me holding my godchild; Great grandmother; Antonio and Rafael Morales, the child's uncles, who have worked with Tumi since 1979. Otavalo, Ecuador, 1987.

working all hours of the day and night. We ran an unsuccessful market stall in Plymouth where we lived and every weekend I had to drive all the way to London to run another stall. At night, the unsold sweaters in the back of my old diesel van became my mattress and the ponchos my blankets. It was a difficult time. Nevertheless, all my suffering and hard work was to be rewarded by the fact that I would soon be back in South America. And travelling between two continents, dividing my time between Britain and Latin America was, as Tumi developed, to become the pattern of my life.

The more I travelled in South America, the more people I got to know. Gradually, my Spanish became good enough to get by in most places. Only in isolated villages and mostly with elderly people, did I have difficulties. Later, I even managed to communicate at a basic level with the older generation in the Inca language, Quechua.

In September 1980 I got to know a group of weavers from the outskirts of Otavalo in Ecuador. The relationship with these Indians, which started out as a trade association, became a close family friendship. I felt exceptionally at home there. Our front man in Ecuador, Antonio Morales, asked me to be godfather to his new-born daughter Miriam, who is now nine years old. That event brought me still closer to the family. And by the early 1980s, I had been given a piece of land, several sheep, and a room in which to stay.

Today, ten years later, I feel perhaps more at home in their village than in my own house in Bath. My arrival is always welcomed by at least two dozen children who escort my car the last part of the journey to the house. And then my goddaughters and godsons all welcome me with hugs and kisses.

While I was visiting a group of artisans in Pisac, Peru, some of them asked me whether I could sell some of their products in the UK such as hand-painted plates and large cylindrical beads. Some of these people, about 15 households, lived a few miles above the Pisac valley in one of the most spectacular geographical locations I have ever seen. Nearby there are ancient Inca terraces and dramatic ruins reaching toward the sky. At night, we all lay next to each other under sheepskins, watching millions of stars. The sound of fresh mountain springs hitting the rocks would lull me into a deep and peaceful sleep.

Living there, I became very close to the heads of this community, a husband and wife, thought to be the oldest couple in Peru (page 42). I knew them as Papa and Mama Quinto – Quinto being their surname. They were direct descendants of the Incas and only spoke Quechua, the Inca language. But we didn't seem to need to say anything. I used to get up early to watch them working in the fields. He was well over a hundred years old but still fit and strong.

In 1982 Mama Quinto died from a bad fever leaving little hope for the old man. The following year he went blind and then refused food until he died. I was very saddened by the whole affair – from then on there was nobody to hold my hands and press them tightly when I returned. We used

Demonstration of quipu, the Inca accounting system. Left to right: Señor Yucra, myself and Alejandro Huatta, a local weaver. Lake Titicaca, Peru.

to sit on the edge of the corn fields and he talked and talked to me. I understood only part of what he said.

I suppose part of the reason I developed love and affinity for these people was because they reminded me of the environment in which I was brought up – and they made up for all that was lacking for me in the West. There was harmony between Man and nature. In the West, *Pachamama*, or Mother Earth, is buried in concrete without respect. Here in Latin America you offer your respect to the land which feeds you. Every time you drink *chicha*, 'corn juice', you first drop some onto the earth as a sign of thanksgiving to Mother Earth.

I still visit the community as much as I can and I always make sure that I spend some time sitting by Mama and Papa Quinto's graves, feeling once again their strength and love. In 1984, their great great granddaughter finally got married after having had three children by the same man (it is normal custom for such Inca families to have children first and then get married), and I was invited to hold the privileged position of *padrino* (best man) at the wedding (page 43). Several kilos of coca leaves, 50 guinea pigs and many gallons of *chicha* was my contribution to the proceedings: several days of dancing and drinking with my friends.

Back in 1978, when we had visited Peru for the first time, apart from the Sacred Valley of the Incas and Cuzco, I had become very attached to several islands in Lake Titicaca. One of the islands, Taquile, has a growing population of 2,000 or so. Each of the six communities can be identified by its surname, and each family belongs to one section of the island which is called a suyo. Traditionally, they have grown quinua, potatoes, oca, broad beans and wheat. Any surpluses are bartered with supplies from the mainland or with fish from the nearby floating islands.

Taquile islanders can be distinguished by their colourful costumes (page 78). And it is the men who knit and use the treadle loom to weave shirts for themselves and skirts for the women. The women do not knit at all but use the traditional loom to weave ceremonial belts, ponchos and other enduring textiles (page 66). During the dry season, from May until September, the islanders spend most of their time weaving and knitting clothes, some of which are sold to outsiders, including Tumi. It is during these cold winter months that most of the 13 festivals take place.

During one of my regular visits to the island, I was asked if I could return to be *padrino* to a young man who had been weaving bayeta cloth for Tumi. During the very traditional and spiritual marriage celebrations, coca leaves were read for good luck and we spent all night chewing coca leaves and drinking *chicha*. The ritual meant that I had agreed to become *padrino* and that I promised to return in May 1983 (May 5 is the traditional day for all weddings).

When I did return, on May 5, I was greeted by one of my friends, Alejandro Flores Huatta, who had prepared my costume for the event. We sat on a bench next to the bridegroom for three days and nights. Pure alcohol, coca leaves and vast amounts of food kept us going. Everybody

Blind spinner using Pushka (Quechua for drop spindle). Ayacucho, Peru, 1981.

brought me, as *padrino*, a bottle of alcohol and a handful of coca leaves. My duty was not only to receive all these gifts, but also to look after the bridegroom, take him to the toilet and so on. As his hands were wrapped together for the full three days he was the only one who was not allowed to enjoy the occasion (page 70).

After this event I became closer and closer to some of the islanders and, just as I had been bestowed with privileged titles in Otavalo in Ecuador or Cuzco in Peru, here my name changed from *Señor* Fini to *Compadre* Fini. Today, I have two further goddaughters in Taquile; one is aged six and the other three. My close association with these islanders encouraged me to organise an exhibition in London at the Commonwealth Institute during the Summer of 1985 entitled 'The Weavers of Ancient Peru'. Not only did I have to prepare a book for the exhibition but I also brought two Peruvian weavers to England, one of them being Alejandro Flores Huatta from Taquile (pages 71/78), and the other, my good friend from San Pedro de Cajas, *Señor* Palomino (page 61).

In March 1987 I returned to South America with a motorbike. Lucy (my travelling companion) and I, landed in Santiago with the bike and from there we travelled south, crossing the border to Patagonia in Argentina. It was cold and a 70 mph wind made Patagonia much more hostile than we had imagined. One of our greatest surprises here was coming across the Welsh tearoom, Nain Maggie, near Esquel (page 81). It seemed to be in the middle of nowhere and brought a smile of recognition to our faces. The entire community was originally Welsh and even today, some 300 years later, many of them still identify with their homeland, like the truck driver we met who introduced himself as 'Tom from Cardiff'.

On the subsequent journey, we were rewarded with some of the most fantastic scenery that we had ever seen (pages 82–85). We continued back through Chile to Peru and Bolivia visiting many villages where our artisans lived and worked. The journey, which raised several thousand pounds for Amnesty International, finished in La Paz where we sold the bike.

My experiences of Central America came two years later after my first trip to South America. By this time Mexico was on the edge of economic collapse, the civil war was simmering in Guatemala, El Salvador was closed because of civil war and CIA-backed guerillas had started a war against the newly elected Sandinista government. Everything was new to me, but as usual, I felt quite at home.

As I went back and forth, at least three times a year, I met a great number of Mexican craftsmen, first at the silver mine in Taxco and then to the south and north of the country. Eventually, I had as much affinity with Mexico and the Mexican way of life as I already had with South America and its lifestyle. Once again I fell in love with the land, the people and, of course, the tortillas and beans.

Potter drying bowls before firing. Oaxaca, Mexico, 1982.

Mexican handicrafts are directed more towards metal and pottery than textiles and they are perhaps the best in the New World in both these fields. In virtually every town and village you will come across potters often using methods that date back to the Mayan, Olmec and Aztec traditions. In San Bartolo near Oaxaca, for example, the artisans produce very simple but beautiful pieces of black pottery, all moulded by hand and fired in primitive clay ovens (page 103).

Guatemala makes a great contrast to Mexico with more than half its population being direct descendants of the Mayas. It is much more an Indian country with over 22 different dialects spoken. Among the Indians, Spanish is spoken the least which is a clear sign of how relatively little their lives and culture have changed since pre-colonial times. Even though during the last ten years Guatemala has experienced perhaps the most brutal period in its history, it still remains a generally happy and joyful society and the colourful Guatemalans are some of the best and certainly the most prolific weavers of all time.

Civil war has closed much of the country to

foreign travellers. But when the route to Nebaj was opened again, two years ago, I met up with a friend, Trevor Moyle, and on hired motorbikes we visited some of the former no-go areas, like Nebaj, where activity had been intense during the war (page 110).

The book concludes with a selection of photos taken during the Easter celebrations in Antigua, Guatemala. These celebrations have become a focal point for other countries in Central America and the city literally overflows with families intent on getting a good view of the processions. In the surrounding villages, as well as in Antigua itself, people spend hours, sometimes days, in the streets making painstaking pictures out of coloured sand and flower petals. These are then systematically destroyed by the bearers of the floats who walk over them crushing the designs. Many thousands of people take part, each taking a turn in helping to carry the vast floats which bear effigies of Christ and the Virgin Mary. Incense is burnt and as the bearers walk they sway from side to side, to provide a mesmerising spectacle against a back-drop of colonial architecture (see pages 122/123).

As time has passed, more than a decade since I first set foot in Latin America, I have spent more and more of each year among these people, often finding new products and new artisans as I make fresh journeys of discovery. As my commitment to Latin American culture and crafts has grown, so has my responsibility for hundreds of people – some of them closer to me than my own parents.

Today Tumi trades with nine countries and several hundred families, all of whom I know individually and visit at least once a year. The characters and communities, the mothers and children, the spectacular landscapes and the ancient traditions, they are all part of the great love and respect which is central to my relation-ship with Latin America. On the basis that one picture says more than a thousand words, the photographs in this book serve as an introduction to the Latin American way of life.

My travelling companion Lucy Davies with three jewellers from the same family: Victor Rodríguez Pereyra, Gabriel Rodríguez Pereyra and Fidel Gutiérrez. Taxco, Mexico, 1987.

Ponchos have many uses. Left: Two Otavalan Indians discreetly urinating. Above: Having a nap. Otavalo, Ecuador.

17

Quena (Andean flute) players during San Juan festival, a celebration of the Summer solstice. Agato Community near Otavalo, Ecuador.

Mother and child. Otavalo Market, Ecuador.

Veronica, the oldest daughter of Segundo Morales (weaver) never stops smiling. She is always to be seen with her younger sister. Agato Community near Otavalo, Ecuador.

Young girl carrying her baby brother, one of my godsons. Agato Community near Otavalo, Ecuador.

Alberto Morales, one of five sons weaving a wallhanging on a treadle loom. Agato Community near Otavalo, Ecuador.

Señor Pablo Vera J. in his workshop. Cuenca is the home of the Panama hat. It is commonly believed that Panama hats got their name after the Panama Canal was dug. Merchants sold their hats on the side of the canal to travellers, and so people presumed the hats came from Panama. Chordeleg near Cuenca, Ecuador.

The plaiting of men's hair and the wearing of hats is believed to have been inherited from the times of Tupac Amaru. Otavalo, Ecuador.

25

Samuel Quinatua in his workshop, painting a balsa wood parrot.
Puyo, Ecuadorian Amazon.

26

A group of Indians swim with some balsa trees for seven hours until they reach their houses where the wood is dried and then carved into parrots. They are then sold to other groups who paint them.
Ecuadorian Amazon.

28

Lake Llanganuco, Huascarán, Peru.

Machu Picchu, the Lost City of the Incas. Taken from Intipunko (the gate of the sun). Peru.

A member of the Quilla family making zampoñas (panpipes) to be used during the Huancané festival. Huancané, Lake Titicaca, Peru.

Huancané Festival, Fiesta de la Cruz, originating from Precolombian times when the cross referred to star constellations occurring around the first week in May. This festival is celebrated throughout the Andean world. Today the celebrations also incorporate the Christian cross. Huancané, Lake Titicaca, Peru.

Keeping and eating guinea pigs is a custom which dates back to Inca times when it was a particularly valuable source of meat. Peru.

Lunchtime. Pisac, Peru.

Drinking Chicha (fermented corn beer) which has been made since pre-Hispanic times and is a basic ingredient for any Andean festivity. Cuzco, Peru.

39

Indians in processional costumes dating back to Inca times. Pisac, Peru.

Old couple from Ampay Community, believed to have been the oldest couple in Peru. The man was thought to be about 120 years old when he died. Pisac, Peru.

Wedding of the great granddaughter of the old couple, opposite,
where I had the privilege of being best man.

43

Little girl from Calca, Sacred Valley of the Incas, Peru.

44

Calca couple in traditional dress. Calca, Peru.

Masks are commonly worn during fiestas throughout Latin America. Virgen del Carmen Fiesta, Pisac, Peru.

Masked dancers in Paucartambo. Many different dancing groups take part in this fiesta, each with their own costumes and dance steps. Virgen del Carmen Fiesta, Paucartambo, Peru.

Blind harp player in Calle Hatunrumiyoc with the famous Inca stone with twelve corners. Cuzco, Peru.

Gourd carving by the García family. Cochas, Huancayo, Peru.

51

Spinner at work. Señora Palomino. San Pedro de Cajas, Peruvian High Andes.

Treadle loom. Santa Ana, Ayacucho, Peru.

Woman, child and llama. Cuzco, Peru.

Pot painting by woman from Amazonian Shipibo tribe.
Pucalpa, Peruvian Amazon.

58

The hands of the weaver. Bolivian Altiplano.

Spinner and weaver couple, Señor and Señora Palomino. San Pedro de Cajas, Peruvian High Andres.

A group of Taquile men ploughing the land. Taquile Island, Lake Titicaca, Peru.

Man from Taquile in search of birds' eggs on rocky island in Lake Titicaca, Peru.

Señora Flores Huatta, left, weaving a belt, above, carrying child.
Taquile Island, Lake Titicaca, Peru.

Tarka players during Fiesta of Santiago or Illapa, the Quechua god of thunder and lightning. Taquile Island, Lake Titicaca, Peru.

Drinking pure alcohol during the same fiesta. Taquile Island, Lake Titicaca, Peru.

69

Wedding on Taquile. All marriages take place on May 5 of each year. Taquile Island, Lake Titicaca, Peru.

Children in doorway. Taquile Island, Lake Titicaca, Peru.

Inca drum player. Ampay, Pisac, Peru.

The Incas used knotted strings as their accounting system, known as quipu. In 1989 on my visit to Peru I met an old man who surprisingly enough still uses quipu to keep a record of his animals, crops and the passing of local festivities. Señor Yucra, Taquile Island, Lake Titicaca, Peru.

Mother and children. Taquile Island, Lake Titicaca, Peru.

Zampoña player. Peruvian Altiplano.

Flores Huatta Family. Three brothers married to three sisters. Parents of sisters on the right. Taquile Island, Lake Titicaca, Peru.

Wild horses. Patagonia, Southern Argentina.

My motorbike outside a Welsh tea-house near Esquel, Argentina.

This and the following photograph were taken during my motorbike trip in 1987. Lago Grey, Parque Nacionel del Paine, Southern Chile.

Perito Moreno Glacier, Southern Argentina.

South America is a continent full of contrasts. On the left, a group of business men in La Paz, Bolivia. Above, a group of Tarabuco Indians, Sucre, Bolivia.

Mariachi trumpet player. Taxco, Guerrero, Mexico.

Group of Mexicans waiting for a bus. Oaxaca, Mexico.

Boys swimming in Mar Muerto, near Juchitán, Oaxaca, Mexico.

In ancient and present-day Mexico mask wearers supposedly achieved their inner desires by the wearing of different faces. Guerrero, Mexico.

The highly polished brown bruñido pottery is here being buried in sawdust after which it will turn black. Señor Estéban de la O Ibarra, Guadalajara, Mexico.

Papier maché animal maker. Señor Clemento Luna, Guadalajara, Mexico.

Potter shaping a bird. Oaxaca, Mexico.

In 1943 the Parícutin volcano erupted out of a cornfield covering the village of San Juan. Interestingly enough the only part remaining is the steeple of the church and today the volcano is still active.
San Juan Parangaricutiro, Michoacán, Mexico.

Looking out. Janitzio Island, Michoacán, Mexico.

Card players in market. Oaxaca, Mexico.

Siesta time for basket sellers. Taxco, Guerrero, Mexico.

Wood carver of naïve pieces using a simple chisel and hammer.
Nahualá, Sololá, Guatemala.

The potters of Oaxaca produce their pieces using purely their hands.
Señora Guadaloupe Leon Garciá, Oaxaca, Mexico.

Pots for sale in the Sunday market. Chichicastenango, Guatemala.

Young girls carrying water from the lake. Santiago Atitlán, Guatemala.

Indigenous women in market. Sololá, Guatemala.

Couple from Todos Santos, near Huehuetenango, Guatemala.

Young weaver. Todos Santos, near Huehuetenango, Guatemala.

Above and cover: Young girl from Nebaj, Guatemala.

Three girls standing by one of the two motorbikes a friend and I hired to travel round Guatemala. Chajul, Guatemala.

Native girls practising basketball. San Antonio Aguas Calientes, Antigua, Guatemala.

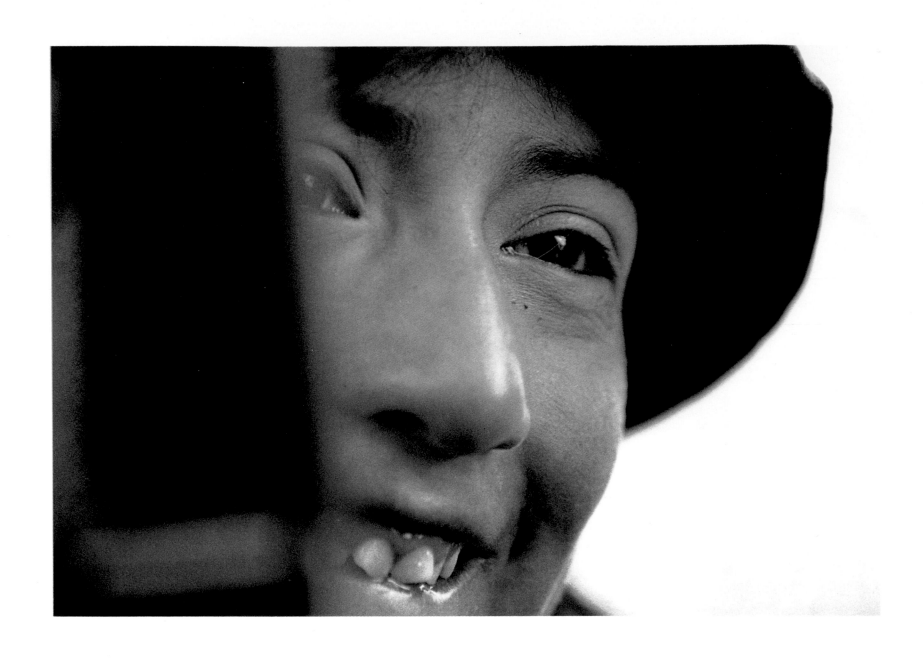

San Cristóbal, Totonicapán, Guatemala.

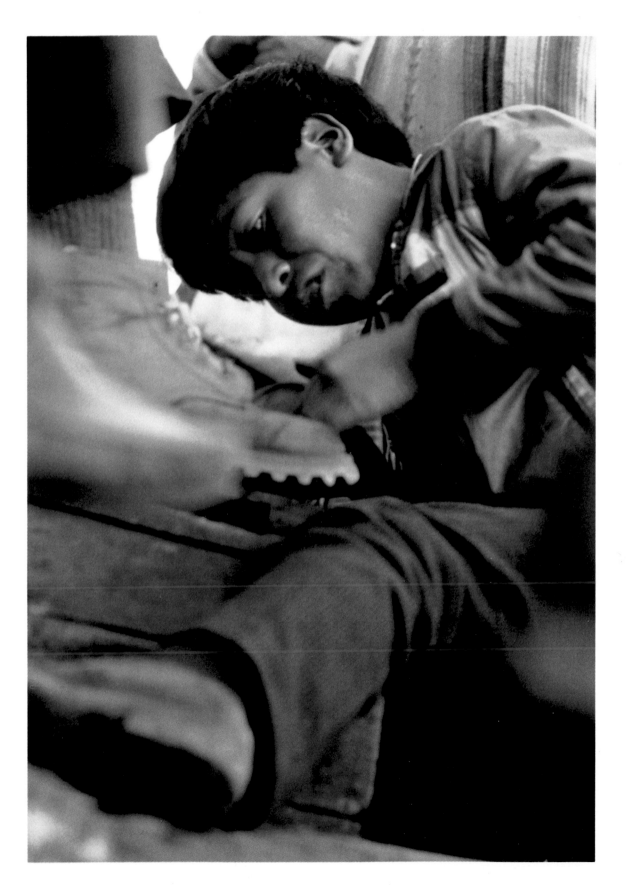

Shoe shining, Totonicapán, Guatemala.

Father and sons, peasant farmers. Todos Santos, near Huehuetenango, Guatemala.

Man from Todos Santos, near Huehuetenango, Guatemala.

Trumpet players during Easter Bank Holiday Celebrations, Antigua, Guatemala.

Mayan marimba player at Sunday market, Chichicastenango, Guatemala.

Antigua has become the centre of Easter celebrations for Central America. Vast processions fill the streets carrying floats with catholic effigies. Here, the mayor's wife plays a prominent role. Antigua, Guatemala.

Mayor carrying float. Following page: Main square, Antigua during the Easter celebrations.